I Am a Good Citizen

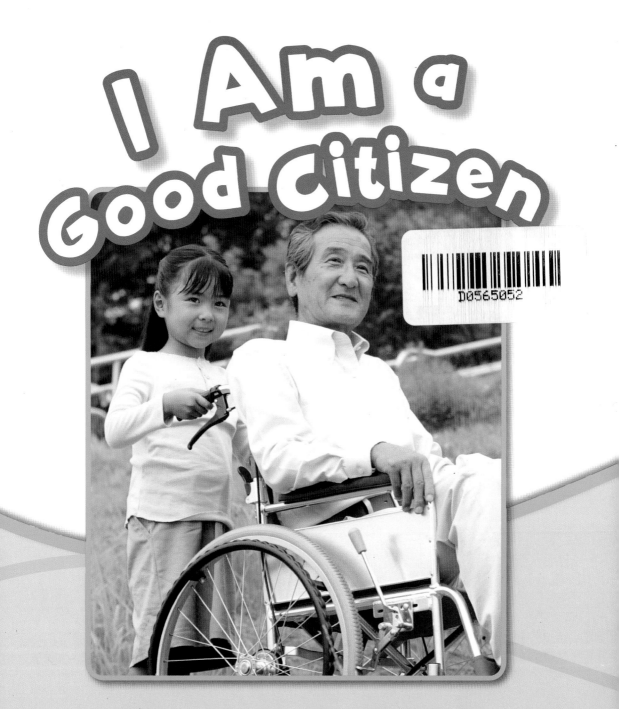

Sharon Coan, M.S.Ed.

I am a good **citizen**.

I do what 'town.

I want to help.

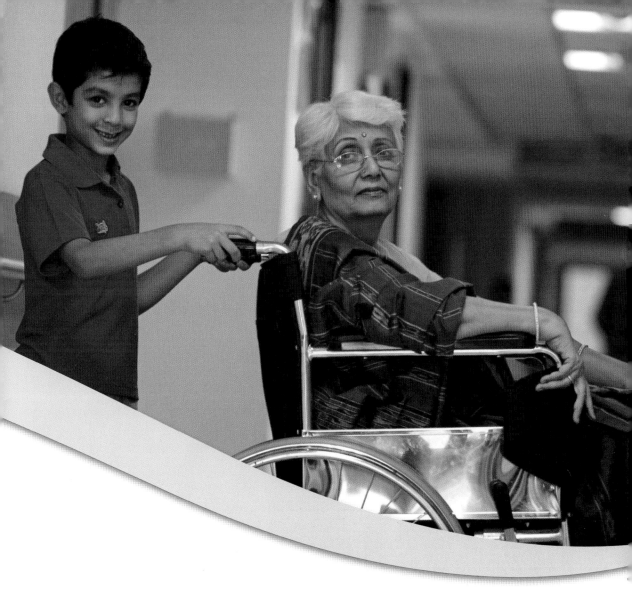

I ask what I can do
to help.

I pick up trash.

I keep my town clean.

I care for others.

I am kind.

I follow the **rules**.

I wait in line.

I follow the **laws**.

I wear a helmet.

I do what is right.

I am a good citizen.

Try It!

1. Talk about ways to be a good citizen.

2. Choose one thing to do.

3. Do it.

4. Tell about it.

Glossary

citizen—a member of a country

laws—rules for the country

rules—things that tell you what you may or may not do

Index

Your Turn!

How can you be a
good citizen? Draw
a picture. Share it
with others.

Consultants

Shelley Scudder
Gifted Teacher
Broward County Schools

Caryn Williams, M.S.Ed.
Madison County Schools
Huntsville, AL

Publishing Credits

Conni Medina, M.A.Ed., *Managing Editor*
Lee Aucoin, *Creative Director*
Torrey Maloof, *Editor*
Lexa Hoang, *Designer*
Stephanie Reid, *Photo Editor*
Rachelle Cracchiolo, M.S.Ed., *Publisher*

Teacher Created Materials
5301 Oceanus Drive
Huntington Beach, CA 92649-1030
http://www.tcmpub.com
ISBN 978-1-4333-7344-2
© 2014 Teacher Created Materials, Inc.